art in
action²

First edition for the United States, its territories and dependencies, and Canada published in 2010 by Barron's Educational Series, Inc.

Copyright © 2010 Elwin Street Productions
Conceived and produced by Elwin Street Productions
144 Liverpool Road
London N1 1 LA
United Kingdom
www.elwinstreet.com

All inquiries should be addressed to:
Barron's Educational Series, Inc.
250 Wireless Blvd.
Hauppaugue, NY 11788
www.barronseduc.com

ISBN-13: 978-0-7641-4441-7
ISBN-10: 0-7641-4441-3

Library of Congress Control Number: 2009940229

Printer Reference Number: 998809/0110/Singapore

The activities described in this book are to be carried out with parental supervision at all times. Every effort has been made to ensure the safety of the activities detailed. Neither the author nor the publishers shall be liable or responsible for any harm or damage done allegedly arising from any information or suggestion in this book.

Picture credits

Edouard Manet, *The Balcony*, The Art Archive/Musée de Louvre Paris,/Gianni Dagli Orti, 12; unknown artist, *The Rainbow Portrait*, Queen Elizabeth I, Hatfield House, England, UK, 18; Amedeo Modigliani, *Anna Zborowska, Lady Wearing a Collar*, The Art Archive/Galleria d'Arte Moderna Milan/Alfredo Dagli Orti, 24; Barent Avercamp, *Winter Landscape*, Hamburger Kunsthalle, Hamburg, Germany/The Bridgeman Art Library, 32; Paul Cézanne, *Mont Sainte-Victoire*, The Detroit Institute of Arts, USA/Bequest of Robert H. Tannahill/The Bridgeman Art Library, 38; James Abbott McNeill Whistler, *Nocturne in Blue and Silver: The Lagoon, Venice*, Museum of Fine Arts, Boston, Massachusetts, USA/Emily L. Ainsley Fund/The Bridgeman Art Library, 44; Paolo Uccello, *St George and the Dragon*, National Gallery London, UK/The Bridgeman Art Library, 52; Flemish School, *Head of Medusa*, The Art Archive/Galleria degli Uffizi Florence/Gianni Dagli Orti, 58; Jacob Peter Gowy, *The Fall of Icarus*, The Art Archive/Museo del Prado Madrid/Alfredo Dagli Orti, 64; Caravaggio, *The Supper at Emmaus*, The Art Archive/National Gallery London, UK/John Webb, 72; Franz Marc, *Im Regan (Under the Rain)*, The Art Archive/Städtische Galerie im Lenbachhaus Munich/Alfredo Dagli Orti, 78; Giuseppe Pellizza da Volpedo, *Flowers in a Meadow*, The Art Archive/Galleria d'Arte Moderna Rome/Alfredo Dagli Orti, 84.

Art Director: Simon Daley
Original photography: Ian Garlick

Printed in Singapore
9 8 7 6 5 4 3 2 1

art in action²

Introducing children
to the world of art with
creative projects inspired
by masterpieces

Maja Pitamic

BARRON'S

Contents

6 **Art and children**

9 **Introduction**

10 **Chapter 1: Portraits**

A snapshot
12 Edouard Manet, *The Balcony*
14 Project Balcony picture box
16 Project Pop art

Rainbow portrait
18 Unknown, *The Rainbow Portrait*
20 Project Oil painting
22 Project Frame

Portrait of Anna
24 Amedeo Modigliani, *Portrait of Anna Zborowska*
26 Project Collage portrait
28 Project Shape a face

30 **Chapter 2: Landscape**

Winter wonderland
32 Barent Avercamp, *Winter Landscape*
34 Project Snow jar
36 Project Medallion picture

Magical mountain
38 Paul Cézanne, *Mont Saint-Victoire*
40 Project Box sculpture
42 Project Watercolor picture

City by night
44 James Abbott McNeill Whistler, *Nocturne in Blue and Silver*
46 Project Misty scene
48 Project Japanese painting

50 Chapter 3: Myths & legends

Fighting the dragon
52 Paolo Uccello *St. George and the Dragon*
54 Project Dragon story box
56 Project Mosaic dragon

Snake hair
58 Unknown, *Head of the Medusa*
60 Project Medusa mask
62 Project Monochrome Medusa

Melted by the sun
64 Jacob Peter Gowy, *The Fall of Icarus*
66 Project Light and sun stained glass
68 Project Flip book

70 Chapter 4: Light & shade

Shock & surprise
72 Michelangelo Merisi da Caravaggio, *The Supper at Emmaus*
74 Project Fabulous fruit
76 Project Sight drawing

Rainy day
78 Franz Marc, *Im Regen (Under the Rain)*
80 Project Giant flowers
82 Project Futurist scene

Field of flowers
84 Giuseppe Pellizza da Valpedo, *Flowers in a Meadow*
86 Project Clay candleholder
88 Project Nature picture

90 Artist biographies
93 Glossary
95 Where to see the art in this book
96 Index

Art and children

by Mike Norris

Can you remember the first time you tried to be an artist? For me it was when I was nine or ten, creating art that was taught by a teacher who seemed more interested in the class remaining orderly than in her students having fun. But I did have fun, though it was a rather secret kind of fun. I never dreamed that I might create art outside of the school curriculum or that my parents might create art with me at home. For one thing, how would we go about it? Well, now there is a way.

Like its predecessor, *Art in Action*[1] for a younger age group, *Art in Action*[2] encourages children (ages nine and over) and family members to learn about art while having fun together in a hands-on creative way. It includes a wide range of pictures, including some very dramatic images, such as the startled head of Medusa, which would perhaps be too scary for a five-year-old child, but is just right for a nine-year-old!

The carefully crafted activities do not ask family artists to slavishly copy works of art by using the same exact materials and techniques the original artists used. In keeping with the skill set of non-professional artists of varying ages, the activities use a wide variety of media that still manage to provide insights into the techniques and lives of the featured artists. Examples include producing three-dimensional versions of paintings and flip books inspired by art works that are hundreds of years old. Some art activities serve as starting points for further projects, such as creating your own version of a portrait of Elizabeth I and then framing it, or making fruit out of newspapers and then drawing them in a still life study. All of the activities are manageble and fun, and all of them will enhance your family's enjoyment and understanding of art.

Mike Norris has been a staff educator at The Metropolitan Museum of Art for over fifteen years and oversees the teaching in the Met's programs for families at the Main Building in Manhattan.

Introduction

The desire to create is innate—from the earliest cave paintings through to the art of today. Indeed, without exception, every child I have taught has wanted to make their mark via art. Children are drawn to the wonders and beauties of the world around them, and their art is a way of engaging with that world.

The four- and five-year-olds that I currently work with love to make sketches from the paintings in the galleries we visit. They appear to have no fear of their work being observed. But with older children, self consciousness seems to creep in. Galleries can sometimes be intimidating places with seemingly perfect pictures on the walls, so I like to remind my students that some of those paintings were produced over many years and some artists had real challenges to overcome. Children really connect with this because every day of their lives, they too are faced with challenges. So I would urge parents to encourage, engage, share, and enjoy artistic endeavors with your children. Along the way, you will learn a lot about them and how they perceive the world.

This book is intended as an introduction to the world of art to share with your child. Don't worry if you've never even set foot in a gallery before because each painting comes with a short introduction, possible questions arising from that painting, and art projects inspired by the painting. Although *Art in Action* is arranged in chapters, there is no set way of using this book. Just let your child dive straight in and pick the painting that most appeals to them. I hope that this will be your start together into the world of art.

A note on art supplies and preparation

- All of the art supplies listed in the activities in this book should be easily obtainable from supermarkets, art stores, and hardware stores.
- Before you start any art activity, it is advisable to cover the area you are working in with a waterproof sheet.
- It is probably a good idea to wear an old T-shirt before activities get messy.

1 Portraits

If you were asked what artists are trying to show in portraits, you would probably answer, "They try to capture the likeness of the sitter and maybe something of their character." But out of the three portraits in this chapter, probably only one fits that definition— can you spot which one? Portraits are about much more than a straightforward likeness of a person. In Manet's *The Balcony*, we can see a snapshot of Parisian life. In the portrait of Queen Elizabeth I, an image of monarchy was presented to the people, and Amedeo Modigliani used the influence of African masks to create a mask-like portrait.

A snapshot

When Edouard Manet's *The Balcony* was exhibited in Paris in 1869, it caused a storm of protest. One art critic thought that it was "gross art". Our twenty-first-century eyes can't see anything in this painting that could give offense, so why did it provoke such outrage at the time?

What's the story?

People were startled when they first saw this painting because of its modern subject matter. People were used to seeing paintings about grand people and events from history, not ordinary, modern-day people. *The Balcony* is a snapshot of Parisian life observed with a cool and detached air. Each person in the picture is lost in their own thoughts. *The Balcony* is a world we are not invited into, and this cold feeling is reinforced by the shadowy and mysterious interior, the green shutters, and the ornate ironwork of the balcony that keeps us back from the scene. The people in the picture are not the main focus of the picture. They don't grab any more attention than the things that surround them—this also offended people.

To people in the nineteenth century, the painting looked unfinished and slapdash because of the loose way the paint was applied, rather than being meticulously painted with objects and people clearly defined. This loose style of painting is almost Impressionistic in style, so it is no surprise to learn that Manet was taught this technique by Berthe Morisot, an Impressionist painter. Berthe is the seated figure in the painting. Jenny Claus, a violinist, is the other woman, and she looks almost Japanese (at the time it was very fashionable to collect Japanese art) with her pale face and dark hair. The man is the painter Antoine Guillemet. In *The Balcony*, Manet wanted to reveal how artificial painting of the time had become. This ambition is one of the things that makes Manet's work modern.

The Balcony	
Artist	Edouard Manet
Nationality	French
Painted	1869

Think about. . .

Why was so little attention given to the people in the painting?
Manet was more interested in capturing a snapshot of modern life than he was in painting a detailed likeness of the people on the balcony.

Was the picture painted very quickly?
Manet applied the paint in very loose strokes to give an impression of the scene—a bit like when you see things out of the window of a moving car, and landscapes, people, and objects appear to be blurred.

Manet used only a few colors in this painting. Why?
The use of mostly dark colors gives the painting a detached and enigmatic feeling.

Project **Balcony picture box**

This art activity recreates *The Balcony* in three-dimensional picture-box form. This project will show you how to make a balcony box and two of the figures. You can add other elements, such as wallpaper, pictures, potted plants, or a dog.

1 At one end of the shoebox, draw a rectangle with your ruler. Leave a border of about ½in (1.25cm) all the way round. Cut out the rectangle. Paint the inside and outside of the box black and allow it to dry.

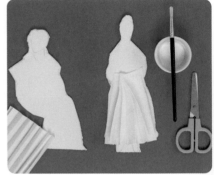

2 Draw and cut out the two female figures. Cut out white tissue-paper tops and glue them on. Fold squares of tissue paper into rectangles, concertina the paper, then stick them on the figures to form the skirts. Color in the faces and hair. Use doily edging on the dresses.

Top tip

You can make your balcony box as three-dimensional as you wish. Put rugs and pictures into the interior, or make the balcony itself with picture wire rather than paper. You could dress your figures in real fabric.

3 Measure and cut out two shutters the length of the box and about 3in (8cm) wide. Paint them and allow them to dry. Cut out long thin strips of card for the balcony railings, make them wider than your shoebox so that you can cut them to fit. Cut out two circles as well, and paint all the railing pieces.

4 Draw a chair on the card, then cut it out and paint it. Secure the chair into the box by using resuable poster putty. Attach the standing figure to the bottom of the box with the putty. Glue the sitting figure into the chair. Use a cocktail umbrella for a parasol and some red tissue for a fan for the seated figure.

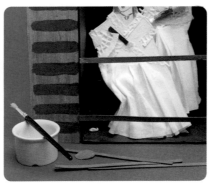

5 Attach a shutter to either side of the shoebox with some clear tape. Measure your piece of green tissue for the top of the box with an overlap of 1in (2.5cm) on three sides. Stick the green tissue paper down on the top of the box.

6 Position all the pieces of the railings on the front of the box, cut them to the exact length, and secure them on with PVA glue.

Project **Pop art**

This next art project takes a detail from *The Balcony* and turns it into a pop art image. Pop art was a style of art that developed in the 1960s. Pop art used techniques taken from advertising and popular culture to produce fine art images. One of the most famous pop art artists was Andy Warhol.

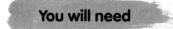
1 Start by taking your ruler and dividing up your 11 x 17in (A3) sheet into six equal squares with your pencil.

2 Wet the sheet with a damp sponge. Then paint each of the squares in a different color or two or three colors in an alternating pattern.

3 While the paint is drying, sketch out the figure of Berthe Moirsot on the printer paper. You can do your own sketch or trace the one on page 13. Trace over the pencil lines with a fine black felt-tip pen and make six photocopies of the image.

4 You can now color in your six figures using your felt-tip pens. You can either color each figure with the same color combination or make each one different. Let your imagination run wild. Cut out each figure and glue one onto each square.

Top tips

• To help you get even squares when you are painting, use your ruler and hold it on the pencil line to make sure you are working along a clean line.
• Allow the squares to dry so the colors don't run into each other and blur the edges.

Rainbow portrait

In order to understand this portrait, you have to put yourself into the minds of Queen Elizabeth I's subjects as they looked at the picture—they believed that God had given Elizabeth a divine right to rule, so she was seen as sacred. This portrait, known as *The Rainbow Portrait*, is not meant to tell us about Elizabeth, it is supposed to tell us about the power of the monarch. The artist has achieved this by putting a series of symbolic images into the picture.

What's the story?

This portrait was painted between 1600 and 1602, and several artists have been credited with its creation. It was painted when Elizabeth was in her sixties (this was a very advanced age in the seventeenth century), so at once, we know that the artist was flattering the Queen because she doesn't look over sixty. But there was another reason that Elizabeth was portrayed so youthfully. It was believed that her virtue or goodness made her ageless. In her hand she holds a rainbow, and above it, there is a Latin inscription, *non sine sole iris*, which means "no rainbow without the sun." Elizabeth, resplendent in her golden orange dress, is the symbolic sun. It has been suggested that the rainbow is a reference to the story of Noah when the rainbow appears as a symbol of hope. The sun helps to make the rainbow, bringing hope to Elizabeth's subjects. On the sleeve of her gown is the serpent of wisdom, and on the rest of her dress, you can see eyes and ears to show that she sees and hears all that goes on in her kingdom. On her collar, there is a jeweled badge displaying her title *Fidei Densor*, which means "Defender of the Faith." On her head, she wears a headdress covered with jewels, and there are pearls around her neck. This portrait was a piece of propaganda, created to remind people of the might of their Queen.

The Rainbow Portrait

Artist	unknown
Nationality	unknown
Painted	1600–1602

Think about. . .

Is this picture a good portrait if it doesn't reveal anything about Elizabeth's character?
The artist never intended to show Elizabeth's character. He wanted to illustrate the majesty and power of Elizabeth as Queen.

What is Elizabeth meant to represent?
Elizabeth is meant to be the sun bringing hope (represented by the rainbow) to her people.

Why does Elizabeth have a serpent on her sleeve and eyes and ears all over her dress?
These are all symbols of her queenship. People of the time would have recognized and understood these symbols.

NON SINE SOLE
IRIS.

19

Project **Oil painting**

The art project inspired by *The Rainbow Portrait* has been spilt in two. The first activity recreates Elizabeth's portrait using home-made oil paints. In the second project you can make a frame for the portrait.

1 Start by lightly sketching in the outline of the portrait.

2 Mix up some flesh tones by adding a few drops of vegetable oil to the powder paints to make a creamy paste. Apply to the paper.

3 Now paint in the rest of the block colors. When the paint is dry, add in the details, including the rainbow and the gold highlights.

4 When the whole painting is dry, use the glue to stick down the pearl barley to represent Elizabeth's pearl necklace and the crystals for her jewels. Allow to dry. Now go on to the frame project on the next page.

Project **Frame**

The frame of a royal portrait was very important. The frame would usually be carved from wood and then be covered in gold leaf (very thin sheets of real gold). For this project, we won't be using gold leaf but a mixture of dried pasta and pretend jewels on a wooden frame, painted gold.

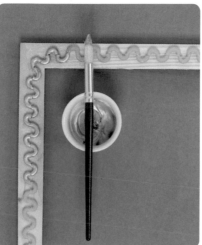

You will need

A plain wooden frame that will fit the previous portrait

Dried pasta (small tubes or bow shapes)

PVA glue

A medium paintbrush

Gold or silver poster paint

A selection of pretend mini jewels

1 Arrange the pasta around the frame so that it forms a continuous pattern. When you are happy with your arrangement, glue the pasta down.

2 When the glue is dry, paint the frame and pasta in gold or silver.

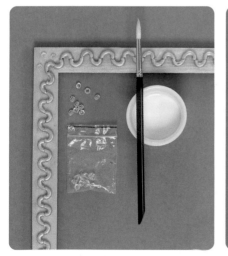

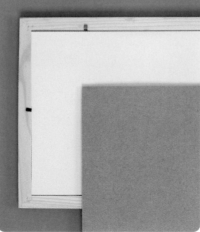

Top tips

• You don't just have to use a frame that is a rectangle. You could use something like an oval, which was very popular during the seventeenth century, but check that it fits your portrait.

• If you want to use this idea to frame a modern picture, then you can leave out the decoration and just paint the frame in a color that you think will match best with your picture.

3 When the paint is dry, decorate with mini jewels. Glue the jewels down and let them dry.

4 Put your royal portrait inside the frame.

Portrait of Anna

We think of a normal portrait as being a likeness of an individual. But when we look at Amedeo Modigliani's portraits, they all seem to have the same characteristics—elongated faces, eyes, and lips, and curving limbs that give the sitter's bodies a sense of movement. Modigliani also tended to use mostly earthy colors, such as browns and yellows, so many of his pictures have the same tone. Yet, despite this repeated style, we get a very clear idea of the individual character of Anna Zborowska from her portrait. How did Modigliani achieve this, and why did he paint his portraits with such recognizable characteristics?

What's the story?

Modigliani was born into a cultivated Jewish family in Livorno, Italy, in 1884. Encouraged by his mother in his art studies he moved to Florence, then Venice, and finally to Paris in 1906. In Paris he met a group of avant-garde artists, including Pablo Picasso and Constantin Brancusi, who looked beyond Western art for their inspiration. Brancusi introduced Modigliani to African masks and sculpture, and this was to be one of the strongest influences on his art. If you look at the *Portrait of Anna*, you can see that she has an oval, mask-like face. In 1917 Modigliani met Leopold Zborowski, a Polish poet who became his art dealer. Zborowski championed Modigliani's work and commissioned a portrait of his wife, Anna Zborowska. The portrait displays all of Modigliani's trademarks; a simple composition, drawn with a few warm colors to create an intimate atmosphere. Anna's collar frames her face, and her hair sits like a cap on her head. But her face reveals nothing, creating an air of mystery. Modigliani depersonalized his portraits, but at the same time, he tried to paint the essence of things so that his art would reach beyond a particular time and place.

Portrait of Anna Zborowska

Artist	Amedeo Modigliani
Nationality	Italian
Painted	1917

Think about. . .

Anna Zborowska's face looks like a mask. Was this intentional?
Yes, it was due to Modigliani's study of African masks.

If you painted this picture using bright colors, how would this change the painting?
Using bright colors would alter the whole mood of the painting. Bright colors would also change the balance of the painting as the outlines in the portrait would no longer dominate the picture. You might like to try this out yourself to see the difference it makes.

Project **Collage portrait**

This art project recreates the *Portrait of Anna Zborowska* in the form of a collage using assorted papers including newspaper, brown paper, and magazine pages.

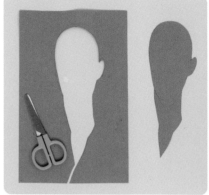

1 On the white paper, draw a line with your pencil that divides the paper in two columns. Find magazine pages similar to both the yellow and red sides of Modigliani's painting, tear them into long strips. Glue the strips into blocks on each side of the paper.

2 On the brown paper, draw and cut out Anna's face and neck. Then stick it down on top of the yellow and red collage background.

You will need

A sheet of white heavy paper, 11 x 17in (A3) or any size

A pencil

A magazine

A glue stick

A sheet of brown paper

A pair of scissors

A sheet of black paper

A doily

A small piece of silver foil

Coloring pencils

4 Now cut out pieces of a doily to create Anna's collar and stick them around her neck and shoulders.

5 For the brooch, cut out an oval from a magazine page and stick it down. Take your silver foil and roll it to make a thin straw. Then stick it down to form the surround of the brooch.

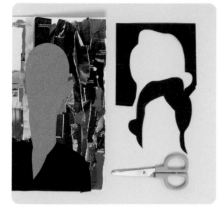

3 Draw the shoulders on the black paper. Then cut out and stick onto the collage paper, joining them up with the neck. Repeat this step for Anna's hair and place it a little way down her head.

6 Finally, sketch in the face and then color it in using your colored pencils.

Project **Shape a face**

In this project, the *Portrait of Anna Zborowska* is recreated using a variety of paints and painting techniques. The paint is applied in stages. By working in this way, you will come to see how Anna's portrait was made up of a series of clearly defined shapes.

1 Begin by sketching an outline of Anna's portrait. Then paint in the background blocks of yellow and red and leave them to dry.

4 Using your fine paintbrush, paint in the flesh tones and the rest of the portrait in sections of plain colors. Allow to dry.

You will need

A sheet of 11 x 17in (A3) white heavy paper or any size

A pencil

Poster or powder paints in similar colors to Anna's portrait

A thick paintbrush

Black watercolor paint or watery powder paint

A sponge

Containers to mix paint

A fine paintbrush

A sheet of black paper, larger than 11 x 17in (A3)

A glue stick

2 With a damp sponge, apply a layer of thin black watercolor paint to the background (the first layer of paint should still show through) and allow to dry.

3 Mix up a darker yellow to match the stripes in Anna's portrait and apply it to the yellow block with a dry brush so the paint is applied evenly. Allow to dry.

5 Now add in the details such as the facial features and the light and shade. Allow the paint to dry between each application.

6 When the painting is dry, glue your finished painting onto a larger sheet of black paper to create a simple frame.

Top tips

• Take time to mix up the paint and get the right shade.
• When sketching out the portrait it helps to think of Anna's face as a series of clearly defined shapes, such as an oval for her head and a cylinder for her neck.
• Note the sharp outline of her face and neck.

2 Landscape

The paintings chosen for this chapter give a very small sample of just how differently landscapes can be portrayed, both in terms of style and in the materials used. In Barent Avercamp's *Winter Landscape* there are many detailed figures at work and at play. In Paul Cézanne's picture, nature dominates in a haze of color, and in Whistler's painting, the buildings of Venice merge into the background, evoking a mysterious mood.

Winter wonderland

When we look at this landscape by Barent Avercamp we enter into his world. The painting's tiny dimensions and circular shape almost suggest that the scene is being viewed through a telescope. It is a closely-observed world full of lively people enjoying winter activities.

Winter Landscape	
Artist	Barent Avercamp
Nationality	Dutch
Painted	17th century

What's the story?

Barent Avercamp, like his uncle the artist Hendrick Avercamp, lived most of his life in Kampen in the Netherlands. It is believed that he studied and trained with his uncle. Indeed, Barent's paintings show such a close similarity to his uncle's that for many years they were attributed to Hendrick and not to him.

Like his uncle, Barent explored the same theme of winter landscapes featuring people at play. In addition to Barent's trademark detailed observation, what marks out this particular landscape is its size; it measures only a little more than 3in (8cm) across, making it slightly smaller than the length of a playing card. This picture is called a medallion, and it was painted in oil paints on a wood panel. It is extraordinary how much detail Avercamp managed to pack into such a small area. The circular shape of the picture increases the illusion of perspective, giving the image an even greater sense of depth.

Avercamp painted a scene of a port. Ports were very important places to the Dutch because they were a great exploring and trading nation. Winters were much colder in the seventeenth century, causing rivers to freeze over for long periods of time, and so life was continued in all its aspects on the frozen ice. The figures at work and at play are painted in dark colors with splashes of red to enliven them. This kind of painting became very popular, possibly because it presented a world that was comfortable and happy, without any harsh realities.

Think about...

What effect does the circular shape of the painting have?
It gives the picture a greater sense of depth, producing a tunnel-like effect.

Why did Avercamp paint most of the figures in dark colors?
If he had painted them in lighter colors they would not stand out so clearly against the ice and a lot of the detail would have been lost.

Why did Avercamp set his painting in a port?
The Dutch were an important trading nation and so ports were very much a part of Dutch life.

"The people are so tiny they look like little insects. I like that boy's sled."
Lucy, age 10

Project Snow jar

Have you ever wondered how they get the snow inside a snow globe? In this next project, you will discover how to do this so that you can create your own winter landscape.

1 Take your piece of the Sticky Tack, mold it into a disk, and put it in the bottom of the jar. The tack will represent the ice.

4 Pour the water into the jar and add about two teaspoons of glycerine and five teaspoons of glitter.

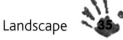

2 On your paper, draw a skating figure or whatever you want to choose from Avercamp's painting—remember that your picture needs to be small enough to fit in the jar. Put your plastic over the drawing and trace your drawing with the marker.

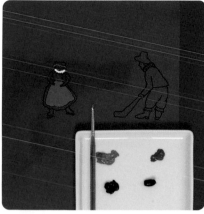

3 Paint your figures on the plastic and allow them to dry. Cut out the shapes, leaving a long strip at the top of the figures to attach them to the top of the jar with.

5 Using tape, stick your cut-out figures onto the inside of the jar lid.

6 Screw the lid back on and secure with a tight rubber band. Shake to watch the snow fall.

You will need

A screw-top jar with as wide an opening as possible

Some reusable poster putty

A sheet of 8½ x 11in (A4) paper

A pencil

A piece of transparent plastic (the type that food containers are made from), not too thick

A black permanent marker pen

Acrylic paints

A fine paintbrush

A pair of scissors

Water

A teaspoon

Glycerine, available from the pharmacy

Silver or white glitter

Clear tape

A rubber band

Project **Medallion picture**

In this art project, we are going to reproduce the content and format of Barent Avercamp's winter medallion picture. We will combine the colors used in the sky to add the figures and fine details throughout the rest of the painting.

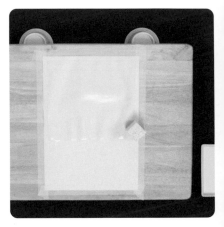

1 Mix the paint: make the yellow runny, the blue slightly thicker, and the gray thicker still. Tilt your board and use a sponge to cover two-thirds of the page with yellow paint, starting from the top.

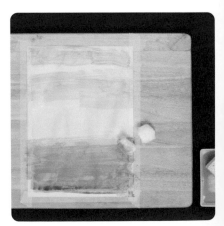

4 Take a piece of cotton wool and while the paint is still wet, dab and twist it over the clouds to give a fluffy appearance.

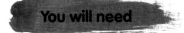
2 Using your other sponge, apply the blue color to the final third of the paper. The color will probably be darker at the bottom of the sheet because of the tilt of the board.

3 Lay the board flat and rinse out the blue sponge. Use it to apply the gray paint to make thick clouds in random streaks all over the sheet.

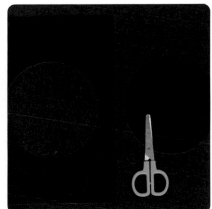

5 Mix all three colors together in a small container. When the sky is dry place your plate in the center and draw around it with your pencil. Using the combined color, paint the figures and other details.

6 To make a simple frame, take the folded black piece of paper, which, when folded, needs to be the same size as your picture, and use the plate to make a circle in the middle. Cut out the circle. Fill in your picture.

Top tips

• It is important to work quickly when painting the sky, to finish before the paint dries.
• On a spare piece of paper, make some sketches of the buildings and figures you are going to draw.

Magical mountain

Some of the artists in this book, such as Caravaggio (see page 72), were noted as geniuses from the moment they picked up a paintbrush, but not even Cézanne's closest friends saw any talent in his early work, and it was dismissed as unimportant. For Cézanne, art was a continual struggle to try to express and understand the relationship between forms (the way that objects look next to each other).

Mont Sainte-Victoire	
Artist	Paul Cézanne
Nationality	French
Painted	c.1904–1906

What's the story?

Cézanne's early attempts at painting were an effort to understand the nature of forms. It was one of Cézanne's friends, the Impressionist painter Camille Pissarro, who showed him Impressionist painting techniques that allowed Cézanne to explore the effects of light in pictures. But ultimately Cézanne came to the conclusion that capturing an impression was not what he wanted to do in his pictures because he worked too slowly. Cézanne decided that his art was about recording his feelings while he was standing in front of nature. "There are no straight lines in nature," he said, "Straight lines are imposed by the artist." Cézanne then worked at depicting a three-dimensional world on a two-dimensional canvas, "The main thing in a picture is to achieve distance. I try to render perspective solely by means of color." This is what we see Cézanne doing in *Mont Sainte-Victoire*—he built up layers of color in planes and modeled objects with color to give the scene a three-dimensional appearance. Color is the unifying force that seamlessly brings together the other elements of Cézanne's composition and forms the picture into one harmonious whole. Cézanne tried to paint the essence of an object, such as what makes a tree look like a tree, so that he could capture a moment suspended in time.

Think about. . .

The colors seem blurred together. Was this intentional?
Yes, for Cézanne colors were a unifying force that held all other elements in a painting together.

The Impressionists' paintings were also blurred. Was Cézanne also trying to capture an impression?
Cézanne was not trying to capture a fleeting moment but trying to reveal the true essence of the subject he was painting.

The painting's composition seems very simple. Was there a reason for this?
By breaking his composition down into simple forms, Cézanne hoped to reveal all of the relationships between them.

Project **Box sculpture**

Cézanne believed that artists should draw and paint nature by the cylinder, the sphere, and the cone with everything in proper perspective, so that each side of an object is directed towards a central point. This sculpture is all about making shapes and about the importance of shape in a composition.

You will need

An assortment of empty boxes

A pair of scissors

Masking tape

PVA glue

Acrylic paints in similar shades to Cézanne's painting

A medium paintbrush

1 Choose a box as your main structure—preferably a rectangular box with a top-opening lid. Cut off the corners of the remaining boxes to make triangular pieces and set aside.

2 Reshape the box—press it down so the sides buckle, lift the lid, and squeeze a corner. Cut a diagonal down one side, repeat on the other side, and extend the cut. Then twist the box around. Tape the box together with masking tape, so that it holds its new shape.

Top tips

• Once you have completed one sculpture, go on to experiment with different shapes.

• Test out colors on a piece of scrap paper to ensure you have the color you want.

• You can achieve a different look depending on the colors you use. Use contrasting colors, like black and white, or complementary colors, such as red and green.

• If you don't have any acrylic paints, just add PVA glue to poster paint.

3 Arrange the triangular pieces around the main box, and when you are happy with the arrangement, glue them on and cover all the joints with tape.

4 When the glue is dry, paint your sculpture using a different shade for each surface. This will emphasize all the different angles of the planes.

Project **Watercolor picture**

When you look at Cézanne's oil painting, the first thing that strikes you is how blurred the image appears. Using watercolors can produce a similar blending of colors, but to give the painting the more solid quality that oil paints have, we are going to cover our watercolor with salt, in order to add a textured finish.

You will need

A sheet of 11 x 17in (A3) white watercolor or heavy paper, or any size you wish

A pencil

A damp sponge

Watercolor paints in similar shades to Cézanne's painting

A medium paintbrush

Salt

1 Place your sheet of paper portrait-way up and roughly sketch out the most important features of Cézanne's painting.

2 Spread water across the paper with the damp sponge until the whole page is covered. Begin painting, starting with the sky and color it with the palest color you can find.

3 Fill in the rest of the background, building up the color from the palest to the darkest. Block in the foreground last.

4 When the painting is complete, and before it has dried, generously sprinkle the salt all over the paper and allow it to dry. When the picture is dry, shake off the excess salt.

Top tips

• Don't make the paper too wet.
• Work quickly while the paper is still wet.
• Have a scrap piece of paper handy to test new colors. This will help you be sure you are happy with the shade.
• Once you have finished you may need to flatten the paper with some heavy books and leave overnight.

City by night

In *Nocturne in Blue and Sliver*, Whistler did not set out to record an accurate picture of the city of Venice. A clue to his intentions lies in the title of the painting. The word nocturne is a musical term that describes a short lyrical piece of music. But the word nocturnal means "of the night," and this is the Venice that Whistler painted. The city emerges through the mist, its lights twinkling seductively, floating like a phantom on the dark water.

What's the story?

James Abbott McNeill Whistler was born in America but spent most of his life in Europe. Whistler went to Venice for practical reasons. In London in 1878, he was involved in a libel case against the art critic John Ruskin. Although Whistler won the court case, he was awarded only a farthing (a quarter of a penny) in damages so he had to declare himself bankrupt. The following year, he was commissioned by The London Arts Society to produce a series of prints of Venice. He stayed in Venice for fifteen months, living in cheap accommodation, having to borrow art materials from other artists. He produced over fifty etchings, ninety pastels, and three oil paintings, of which the *Nocturne* is one.

In the composition and lines of the *Nocturne,* you can see the influence of Japanese art, which was being seen and collected in Europe for the first time. For Whistler, painting was about creating beauty that would "improve on nature." But it was the way Whistler put paint onto canvas that marked him as an influential painter; he applied paint with the utmost delicacy, or as Whistler himself put it, "Paint should not be applied thickly. It should be like a breath on the surface of a pane of glass."

Nocturne in Blue and Silver	
Artist	James Abbott McNeill Whistler
Nationality	American
Painted	1879–1880

Think about. . .

Why are the buildings of Venice difficult to see?
Because Whistler wanted to paint a mood, not buildings.

What mood did Whistler create in the painting?
A mood of mystery and of an other-worldliness.

How did Whistler create his intended mood?
He applied the paint with a very delicate touch and surrounded the city with a mist. We are only aware of the buildings because of their twinkling lights, shining through the half light.

"I think there are pirates in that picture. You can see their ship."

Jordan, age 9

Project **Misty scene**

In this project, the moonlit city of Venice is captured using dark blue paper and a stencil of the city's silhouetted buildings. These elements are combined with a paint-splattering technique that uses an old toothbrush. The finer details are then added after the stencil has been lifted. The paint splattering can be messy, so be sure to cover yourself and your work area before you start.

1 Draw the silhouetted buildings from Whistler's painting onto the white poster board.

2 Cut the buildings out. Place the cut-out shapes onto the colored paper. Secure with masking tape.

3 Make sure the paint is runny. Put the toothbrush in the paint and draw a ruler over the bristles toward you. The paint will splatter away from you. Repeat with another color.

4 When the paint is dry, carefully lift off the cut-out shapes and add details to the buildings. Highlight the reflections on the water with gold or yellow paint.

You will need

A sheet of thin white poster board or heavy paper, 11 x 17in (A3) or any size

A pencil

A pair of scissors

A sheet of dark blue construction paper, 11 x 17in (A3) or any size

Masking tape

Poster or powder paints in pale shades

An old toothbrush

A ruler

Gold or yellow poster or powder paint

Top tips

• Don't overload your toothbrush with paint or it will drip.
• Clean your toothbrush between using different colors.

Project **Japanese painting**

Nocturne in Blue and Silver clearly shows the influence of Japanese art in its technique and composition. Japanese artists use rice paper and colored inks, but we will use textured paper and watercolor paints in this project.

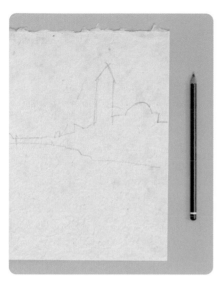

1 Sketch out the buildings of Venice on your white paper.

2 Fill in the buildings with black watercolor paint.

You will need

A sheet of textured white paper, 11 x 17in (A3) or any size

A pencil

Watercolor paints

A medium paintbrush

Gold acrylic paint

3 Gradually build up the other colors using an almost-dry paintbrush.

4 Finally, add the highlights with gold acrylic paint and allow the picture to dry.

Top tip

Remember to use an almost dry paintbrush because the paper might bubble if it gets too wet.

3 Myths & legends

Why have artists through the ages chosen to paint scenes from myths and legends? Probably because myths and legends are filled with exciting plots and superhuman characters so artists can let their imaginations run wild. Paolo Uccello coolly and elegantly portrayed St. George and the dragon, yet we are still drawn to the drama of the scene. The artist who painted the *Head of the Medusa* captured the full horror of the moment. Jacob Peter Gowy showed the dreadful scene when Icarus fell from the sky, his wings melted by the heat of the sun.

Fighting the dragon

In *St. George and the Dragon* Paolo Uccello created a fantastical and decorative world. The figures are elegant, the circles on the dragon's wings and the squares of grass make beautiful patterns. This picture is quite clearly of its time, both in its subject matter and in the costume of the figures, yet, it is just as interesting to modern eyes as it was when it was first seen.

St. George and the Dragon	
Artist	Paolo Uccello
Nationality	Italian
Painted	*c.*1470

What's the story?

St. George and the Dragon was painted toward the end of Uccello's life. The picture was based on a story from *The Golden Legend*, a collection of stories on the lives of the saints. The painting depicts two scenes from St. George's story; the point at which St. George defeats the dragon and the princess is rescued, and also the moment when he uses the princess's belt to tie up the dragon in order to take it into the town. The gathering storm clouds indicate that St. George has the support of divine forces. The focus point of the painting is the tip of St. George's lance as it pierces the dragon. The knight's lance cuts through the picture in a sharp diagonal—in fact, it is the only straight line in the painting. The rest of the picture is composed of curves, spirals, and patterns. The wonderfully undulating horse, with his spiraling tail, is mirrored in the dragon's tail. The colors are cool, except for the carefully balanced use of red. But perhaps the most fantasy-like features of all are the figures of St. George and the princess. Despite St. George's charge against the dragon, they both give off an air of serenity. As for the two-legged dragon, it is hard to believe that this is a beast that terrified a town. He looks more like the princess's tame pet on a leash. Uccello created a magical world that we are fascinated to enter, ensuring that this painting is as appealing to people now as it was when it was created, five hundred years ago.

Think about. . .

The painting is mainly composed of cool colors, such as blues and grays, except for some splashes of red. Why?
The cool colors lend a detached, almost dream-like mood to the painting. The use of red highlights the cool colors further and adds to the decorative elements within the painting.

The painting has lots of curvy and spiraling shapes. Why?
In addition to producing a decorative effect, the spirals put movement into the painting and direct our attention toward the contrasting shape of St. George's straight lance.

"I know the dragon is on a leash, but I think he is still scary because of his teeth and all that dripping blood."

Rosie, age 11

Project **Dragon story box**

This art project takes its inspiration from the story of St. George and the dragon, from *The Golden Legend*. There are two scenes from the story in Uccello's painting, but, in this project, you will be able to incorporate the entire story in a specially-made box. Read the storyboard on page 55 to find out the whole story of St. George and the dragon.

You will need

A small box with a lid approximately 2 x 2in (5cm) square

Decorative jewels

PVA glue

A strip of pale-colored construction paper or heavy paper the same width as the box and about 12in (30cm) long

A pencil

Some coloring pencils or felt-tip pens

A glue stick

1 Decide on a design for the lid of your box; this could be the dragon, St. George, the princess, or simply a pattern. Sketch in your design, color in the lid, and stick on some decoration using PVA glue.

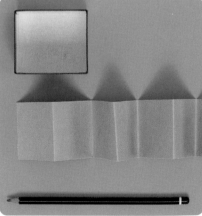

2 Fold your strip of paper into an accordion pattern of squares or rectangles that will fit inside the box. If you follow the measurements given, you should end up with about seven squares with a ½in (1.25cm) of paper left over, which needs to be on the left.

Storyboard

• A country is terrorized by a dragon.
• The dragon is given two sheep a day to eat.
• When the sheep run out, a raffle is drawn for people to be given to the dragon.
• One day the king's daughter is selected.
• The king is allowed seven days until his daughter has to be taken to the dragon.
• As the princess approaches the dragon's cave, St. George appears.
• St. George makes the sign of the cross and "smites" the dragon.
• Using the princess's belt, St. George ties up the dragon. The princess leads it back to the city.
• St. George tells the people that he will kill the dragon if they are baptized.
• A church of St. George is founded. It has a holy well.

3 Decide which part(s) of the story you want to depict. Sketch in the episodes of the story, square by square, working from left to right. Then color in your pictures.

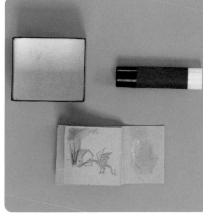

4 Use a glue stick to attach the extra ½in (1.25cm) piece of the story strip to the inside bottom of the box. Fold down the strip and close the box lid.

Project **Mosaic dragon**

This next art project is inspired by the ancient art of *tesserae* or mosaic, where small colored pieces of glass, tile, or stone are set into a floor or wall to make wonderful pictures and patterns. In this project, we are going to use paper to create a mosaic dragon.

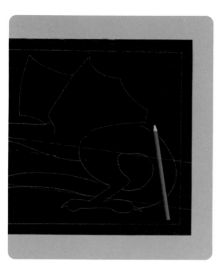

You will need

A pencil

Black construction paper, 11 x 17in (A3) or any size

A ruler

Colored paper, old magazines, paint sample color strips, or tape

A pair of scissors

PVA glue

A medium paintbrush

A small household paintbrush

1 With your pencil, draw a dragon onto the construction paper. Draw a border all the way around the picture with your ruler.

2 Cut up your colored paper into ½in (1.25cm) squares and divide them into piles of the same colors.

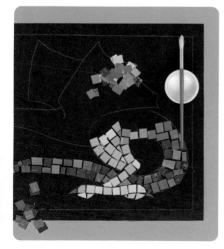

3 Glue the squares onto the paper inside the drawing/border. Leave gaps so that they look like tiles.

4 Mix some PVA glue with water. Paint all over the mosaic to make it shiny. Allow your picture to dry.

Top tips

• If using paint color sample strips, you could use the same color in different shades. This will give your mosaic more of a three-dimensional feel.
• You could also try using colored foil or wallpaper.

Snake hair

The story of Medusa from Greek mythology is one that has fascinated artists throughout the centuries. Artists from Caravaggio to Rubens have used Medusa as a subject for their paintings. This Medusa is now attributed to the Flemish school (c.1620–1630), but for centuries it was thought to be by the artist Leonardo da Vinci. So what makes this version of Medusa so special?

Head of the Medusa	
Artist	unknown
Nationality	Flemish
Painted	c.1620–1630

What's the story?

In Greek mythology, Medusa was a daughter of the sea gods Phorcys and Ceto. Medusa was a mortal woman whom Athena (goddess of wisdom, war, and the arts) changed into a gorgon. Gorgons were vicious female monsters with brass hands, sharp fangs, and living venomous snakes for hair. Anyone looking upon Medusa's face would be turned into stone. Medusa was killed by Perseus, one of the first Greek warrior heroes. He then presented her head to Athena, who placed it on her shield.

The viewpoint of this painting of Medusa is very unusual. Instead of the more common image showing her whole face from the front, Medusa's head is lying on the ground, and we are immediately confronted by a mass of writhing snakes. To add to the drama of the moment, the artist used extreme effects of light and shade, allowing just a slither of light to fall onto one side of her face. A mist comes out of Medusa's open mouth that surrounds her whole head. Through the mist we can seen toads, bats, and other sinister creatures. Despite the writhing snakes, we feel sympathy for Medusa. Her face is plainly human in its obvious fear. We are drawn into her nightmare and share her horror of it. This is what makes this painting and its interpretation of the Medusa story unique.

Think about. . .

Why did the artist show Medusa from an inverted angle?
So that we are immediately confronted by the writhing snakes, adding to the drama.

What effect does the mist have on the mood of the painting?
Things seem to loom out at us through the mist, giving a sinister mood to the painting.

The artist surrounded Medusa with toads, bats, and other creatures. Why?
The other creatures make us aware that Medusa is being observed, and they reinforce the horror of her situation.

"I think all those snakes are really scary."
Scott, age 10

Project **Medusa mask**

Make your own Medusa mask using a balloon, papier mâché, garden wire, and bubble wrap.

1 Blow up the balloon to roughly the size of your head. Then tie a knot in it. Mix the wallpaper paste. Tear the newspaper into small strips. Mix with the paste and then cover half the balloon. Add another layer. Then allow it to dry. Repeat until you have built up about eight layers of papier mâché.

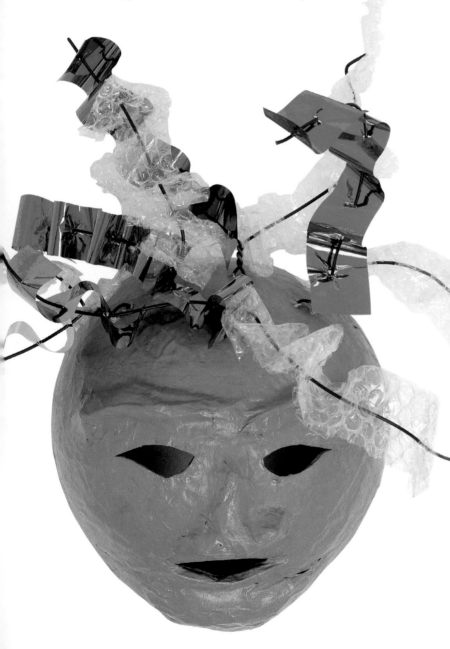

4 Paint the face and allow it to dry. With the craft needles make pairs of holes around the edge of the mask (just above the forehead) where the hair will go. Cut lengths of garden wire with the pliers.

2 Allow the papier mâché to dry out completely, and then pop the balloon to remove it. Trim the edges of the mask, and make eye holes and a mouth with a pair of scissors.

3 Draw the rest of the facial features with a pencil. Scrunch up small pieces of newspaper and stick them on with masking tape to form the nose, eyebrows, chin, and mouth. Add two layers of papier mâché and allow to dry.

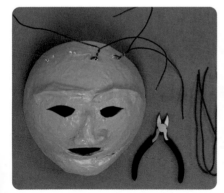

5 Thread a length of wire through each pair of holes. Twist together the wires just above the holes to secure. Bend the wires into snake shapes, then weave through a strip of bubble wrap or shiny foil.

6 Repeat this step with all the other holes and wires. Alternate the materials between bubble wrap and shiny foil. Secure each of the wire ends with clear tape.

You will need

A balloon

Wallpaper paste

Newspaper

A broad paintbrush

A pair of scissors

A pencil

Masking tape

Poster paints

A medium paintbrush

A craft needle

Garden wire, the type used for tying up plants

A pair of pliers

Strips of bubble wrap and shiny foil

Clear tape

Top tips

• Vary the lengths of wire you use for the hair.
• Candy wrappers are a good source of different colors of foil.

Project **Monochrome Medusa**

This next art project uses black construction paper and white string to recreate Medusa's head in black and white.

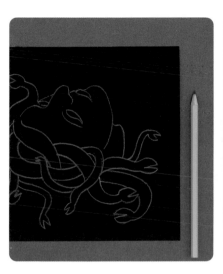

1 Sketch an outline of Medusa's face, neck, and hair of snakes.

2 Paint the PVA glue over a section of the pencil lines.

3 Measure bits of string and cut. Stick them down over the glue lines. Try to use long pieces rather than lots of small pieces. Repeat steps 2 and 3 until all the pencil lines have been covered.

4 Cover your work with a sheet of greaseproof paper and weigh down with some heavy books. Leave overnight. When completely dry, mount the head onto a sheet of white paper.

You will need

A sheet of black construction paper, 11 x 17in (A3) or any size

A pencil

PVA glue

A fine paintbrush

A ball of white string

Scissors

Greaseproof paper large enough to cover the construction paper

A sheet of white paper larger than the construction paper

A glue stick

Top tip

Don't make your sketch too elaborate—the simpler the better.

Melted by the sun

The Fall of Icarus is a painting in the baroque style. Baroque paintings were all about grand theatrical gestures, bold colors, and contrasting lighting. The fall of Icarus was a perfect story for a baroque picture because it contains all of these exciting ingredients. Yet, while we might admire all of these dramatic effects, they are not the real heart of Gowy's painting. The true subject of his picture is our need for freedom and to live our dreams, symbolized by our desire to fly.

The Fall of Icarus	
Artist	Jacob Peter Gowy
Nationality	Flemish
Painted	*c.*1636

What's the story?

The story of Icarus begins with Icarus's father, the architect and sculptor Daedalus. Daedalus built a labyrinth for King Minos of Crete, in which to house the Minotaur, a monster that was half man and half bull. Once Daedalus had built the labyrinth, the king imprisoned Daedalus and Icarus. Daedalus hatched an escape plan. He made two pairs of wings from feathers held together by wax. He handed the wings to Icarus and, as Icarus put them on, Daedalus warned him not to fly too close to the sun, in case the wings melted. They took to the sky, and, delighted by the sensation of flying, Icarus forgot his father's warning and flew too close to the sun. The wings fell apart, and Daedalus was forced to watch his son fall.

The famous artist Rubens made the original sketches for this picture, but it was Gowy who painted the final work. We can see two small figures on the beach, which we assume are Daedalus and Icarus before their flight. The sea is choppy and rough, and the sky is partly overcast. The two bodies create contrasting arcs in the middle of the picture and have contrasting expressions on their faces. The dark, shadowy waters of the sea are the opposite of the shaft of sunlight that lights up Icarus's flesh and exposes his vulnerability as he falls to certain death.

Think about...

What effect does the use of the red scarf have on the rest of the painting?
Put your fingers over the red scarf and notice what happens to the surrounding colors. They appear duller and less intense. The red also focuses our attention on Icarus's falling body.

What do you think Gowy was trying to convey when he painted the feathers surrounding Icarus?
Again this is a question of contrasts. Compare Daedalus's firm, compact wings with Icarus's gossamer-light feathers. These opposites point to Icarus's inevitable fall.

Project **Light and sun stained glass**

In this project, we will use the outline of the single figure of Icarus to produce a piece of work similar in effect to a stained-glass window.

1 Trace Icarus in the center of your tracing paper. Make sure your image is no bigger than 5½ x 8½in (A5). When you are happy with your drawing, go over it with a black felt-tip pen. Draw a circle around it. A plate can be useful for this.

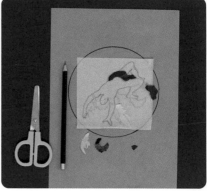

2 Now trace your drawing again, and use this image to transfer the shapes of Icarus onto different colored bits of tissue. Cut the pieces out. Measure out a piece of plastic sheet larger than your drawing and stick it over the drawing with masking tape.

3 Using PVA glue, stick your tissue shapes onto the plastic sheet. You could also add some rays of sunlight.

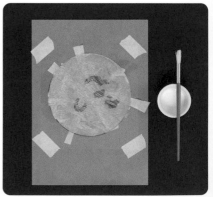

4 Finally, cut a circle of light-blue tissue the same size as the circle that frames Icarus. Glue it exactly over the picture.

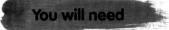
You will need

Tracing paper, 8½ x 11in (A4) in size

A pencil

A black felt-tip pen

A plate to act as a circle guide

Colored tissue in blues, greens, red, brown, yellow, and flesh tones

A pair of scissors

A sheet of clear plastic, 8½ x 11in (A4) in size

Masking tape

PVA glue

A fine paintbrush

Black construction paper, larger than your drawing of Icarus

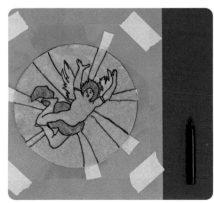

5 Outline the figure of Icarus and the rays of sunlight with the black felt-tip pen.

6 When dry, gently peel the tissue and polythene apart. Make a simple circular frame for your picture using black construction paper. Display on a window.

Top tip

Remember that tissue can tear easily, so handle it with care.

Project **Flip book**

This next art project takes the form of a flip book—
flipping through the pages of the book makes the
static drawings look as if they are moving.

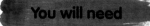

Sheets of 8½ x 11in (A4)
white paper

A pencil

A ruler, metal if possible

A craft knife or scissors

A stapler

Felt-tip pens

1 Start by making up your flip pad. Cut up the large sheets of paper into small rectangles. Keep them all the same size.

2 Staple the paper pieces together on the left-hand side.

3 Decide how much of the story you want to tell in your book. You could start from when Icarus puts on his wings, goes up to the sun, and then falls, or you could just do his descent. It will depend on how many pages are in your book.

4 Make a simple sketch of Icarus on each page, slightly altering the position of his body each time. It's up to you how much detail you want to include. Color the drawings in. Then flip through the book and watch Icarus fly.

Top tips

• Make sure you keep each drawing on the right-hand side of the paper.
• The more pages you have, the more effective your book will be.
• You could buy and use a ready-made pad.

4 Light & shade

How do light and shade play a big part in the composition, mood, and drama of a painting? If you compare the extreme, theatrical light used by Caravaggio in *The Supper at Emmaus* with the bright energetic colors of Franz Marc's *Im Regen* (*Under the Rain*), and the delicate pastel tones used by Guiseppe Pellizza da Volpedo in *Flowers in a Meadow,* you will get some idea of the vastly different results that artists achieve using effects of light and shade in their paintings.

Shock & surprise

Caravaggio's painting has a tremendous dramatic force. *The Supper at Emmaus* shows the moment of revelation when Christ's identity is revealed to the apostles sitting with him. Yet, despite the Christian subject matter of this work, the Church was Caravaggio's fiercest critic. So what was it that made Caravaggio's art so controversial?

What's the story?

Caravaggio's life was as dramatic as his paintings. His terrible temper led to him being continually on the run to escape prison. Caravaggio painted in a style that matched his personality. He painted straight onto the canvas with very little preparation and quickly painted over work he didn't like. Caravaggio introduced a revolutionary realism to art that was shocking in its directness. The apostles were painted as ordinary working men. Only Christ's gesture of blessing reveals his identity. It was this ordinariness that drew such criticism from the Church.

One of the painting's greatest strengths is the way that we are drawn into the action of the scene. The innkeeper looks puzzled by the reactions of the apostles, but we know the secret. Such is the shock created by Christ revealing his identity that it cannot be contained in the space of the picture, but erupts out from the canvas. St. Luke broadly gestures as he recognizes the hand of Christ. St. Matthew's elbow bursts from his jacket. The fruit bowl balances precariously on the table's edge. But perhaps the real scene-stealer in the painting is the light. Caravaggio used light in his paintings in a theatrical way. Christ's shadow reinforces his blessing gesture so that the light in the painting is like the light of truth revealing Christ. Caravaggio transformed the ordinary into the extraordinary, and this is what makes him one of the greatest artists of the seventeenth century.

The Supper at Emmaus	
Artist	Michelangelo Merisi da Caravaggio
Nationality	Italian
Painted	1596–1602

Think about. . .

What emotions did Caravaggio try to capture?
Caravaggio wanted to capture the wonder, surprise, and shock of the apostles at the exact moment that they realize Christ is sitting at the table with them.

How did Caravaggio heighten the drama of the scene?
Caravaggio used extremes of light and shade and contrasted the dramatic gestures of the apostles with the calmness of Christ. He also stretched the natural perspective of the painting, e.g. the jutting elbow, and he let us in on Christ's secret. We are not puzzled by the apostles' reactions, unlike the innkeeper.

"If that's Jesus, then he looks pretty normal in this picture. Just like anyone really."

Bruce, age 11

Project **Fabulous fruit**

This art project focuses on the wonderful still life of the fruit in a bowl that balances precariously at the edge of the table in Caravaggio's painting. You feel that you could reach out and pluck the fruit from the bowl. Such was Caravaggio's skill at making the fruit appear real. We are going to make our own fruit with a combination of paper, glue, and paint.

1 Start by scrunching up your newspaper into different shapes of fruit, any size you want.

2 Tape around the fruit to hold the shapes in place.

You will need

Newspaper

Masking tape

PVA glue

A medium paintbrush

Poster paint or powder paints

Brown pipe cleaners for stalks, cut to fit each fruit

3 Make a mixture of watered-down PVA glue and brush it onto the fruit. Allow the glue to dry.

4 Paint your fruit. Build up the colors and allow them to dry between coats. Put on another layer of watered-down PVA. Allow to dry. Cut the pipe cleaners to fit. Then push in as stalks.

Top tip

The fruit could be used in the next project as props for the still life sketch in pencil.

Project **Sight drawing**

The next art project is all about observing—using your eyes to really look at things. We are going to focus on the still life of the bowl of fruit that is a key feature of Caravaggio's painting. We are going to use the fruits from the previous art project, but if you have not yet made these, you can of course use real fruit. Artists use all sorts of materials for their sketches— pencil, charcoal, graphite. By using monochrome you will come to understand how a composition is held together and also how light and shade help to add depth and drama to a picture.

1 Start by creating a display: select your fruit and arrange it. Add props if you like, such as a plate, napkin, or knife.

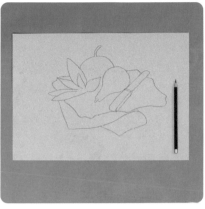

2 Select a 2B pencil. Place your display on a table a few feet away and lightly sketch its outline.

You will need

The 3D fruit from the previous project or fresh fruit

Any other props required, such as a plate, knife, or napkin

Some sheets of mid-tone cartridge or construction paper in cream or gray, 8½ x 11in (A4) or larger

A selection of pencils ranging from 2B to 6B

A piece of chalk

3 Once you are confident you have drawn the basic shape of the fruit, start filling in the details. Look for the darkest areas first, and observe if your still life casts a shadow on the surrounding surfaces. Take care to shade the darkest areas in with the highest number B pencil.

4 Once the dark areas are shaded in, start filling in the lightest areas using the chalk.

Top tips

• When you draw more than one object, you need to consider and compare their proportions.
• Do lots of sketches from different angles and in different kinds of light.
• To achieve a greater contrast between the light and the shadows, you could switch on a desk lamp above your still life.

Rainy day

Have you ever noticed how the rain changes the colors in the landscape? The rain often seems to make colors appear softer and less intense. But in Franz Marc's *Im Regen* (*Under the Rain*), the weather has created a tropical world inhabited by strange people and animals. As the rain falls, the colors glow with intensity.

What's the story?

Franz Marc was born in Germany in 1880 and studied at the Munich Academy of Fine Arts. He traveled to Paris where he was influenced by the work of Vincent van Gogh and Paul Gauguin. He returned to Germany, and, in Berlin, along with Wassily Kandinsky and August Macke, he formed a breakaway art group called the Der Blaue Reiter (The Blue Rider), named after a painting by Kandinsky of a blue rider on a blue horse. The group printed their new ideas about art in the *Der Blaue Reiter Almanac* and held influential exhibitions that invited artists of many different modern styles to come together to show their work to the public.

For The Blue Rider artists, art was powerful only if it directly expressed feelings. Marc was influenced by the modern art styles of Futurism (an Italian art movement interested in the depiction of speed, machines, movement, and modern life) and Cubism (a French art movement that broke down everyday objects and then put them back together again in a slightly disjointed way to represent an object from lots of different angles at the same time), but at the heart of his work was the wish to reveal the spirituality of nature. Marc expressed this spirituality through color. For Marc, colors represented emotions: blue stood for masculinity and spirituality, yellow was femininity and joy, and red represented the sound of violence.

Im Regen (Under the Rain)	
Artist	Franz Marc
Nationality	German
Painted	1912

Think about. . .

Why did Marc call this painting *Under the Rain*?
The title gives Marc the opportunity to show contrasts, such as the driving rain against the bright colors and the strong diagonals against rounded shapes.

Why did Marc use such vibrant colors?
For Marc, color was a means of expressing emotion, with each color representing a different feeling.

If you had to choose colors to express different moods and emotions, what would those colors be and what would they express?
This is entirely your choice. You may like to put down your ideas in another art project.

"I think the red lady is very pretty. Is that her dog?"
Beth, age 9

Project **Giant flowers**

This project tries to capture the vibrant colors of Marc's painting by creating a tropical setting. If you have ever been to a rainforest or seen pictures of one you will know that everything appears larger than life and very lush. These flowers are set against a stormy sky so that their colors appear even more intense.

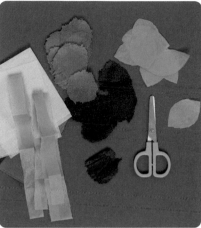

A sheet of 11 x 17in (A3) white heavy paper

A damp sponge

Watercolor paint or watered-down powder paint in blue-gray tones

A paintbrush

Tissue paper in shades of pink, red, orange, and green

A pair of scissors

A glue stick

A fine black felt-tip pen

1 With a damp sponge apply a thin layer of moisture all over the sheet of paper. With your paintbrush add gray watercolor paint in broad sweeping strokes.

2 While the paint is drying, tear or cut up the pink, red, orange, and green tissue paper into petal, stem, and leaf shapes.

3 Arrange the petals, stems, and leaves on the dry sheet. Layer and overlap the tissue petals. Then glue all the tissue pieces down.

4 Make sure the glue is dry. Then take your fine felt-tip pen and add detail to the flowers and leaves.

Top tips

• The more you layer and overlap the tissue, the more effective the flowers will look.
• When you are gluing down the petals, don't glue them down completely. This will give a more three-dimensional effect.

Project **Futurist scene**

This project captures the Futurist style of Marc's work, as well as the hot, intense colors he used in *Im Regen*. To recreate these elements all you need is some old magazines. The effect of the driving rain can be made by cutting up the pictures and setting them in diagonals.

82

1 Select some suitable pictures from the magazines.

2 Cut out your chosen pictures in long thin strips. You may want to use a pencil and a ruler.

You will need

Some old magazines, particularly ones that feature landscapes, people, and animals

A pair of scissors

A pencil

A ruler

A sheet of 11 x 17in (A3) white heavy paper or any size

A glue stick

A piece of black construction paper bigger than your finished picture

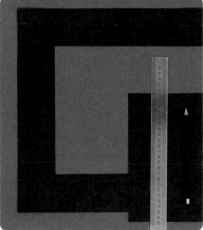

3 Arrange the strips in diagonals onto the white paper. When you are happy with your arrangement, glue down the strips, making sure that there are no gaps.

4 When the glue has dried, make a simple frame for the picture using some black construction paper or any other black paper.

Top tips

• Take time to arrange the paper strips to get a good balance of colors.
• Don't worry if you can't get similar animals or people to Marc's painting. The idea is just to get the feel of bright colors shifting and moving.

Field of flowers

Giuseppe Pellizza da Volpedo was born in the farming town of Volpedo, and despite traveling to the great art centers of Europe, he returned to his home town to live and work. This is the essence of his work; a love of the land where he grew up and a fascination with the way people were tied to the land through their life and loves. This is what we see in his painting *Flowers in the Meadow* —the countryside takes on an almost mystical air, and the two children seem to be folded into the landscape.

What's the story?

Pellizza's work was influenced by the Italian Realist School, and many of his paintings were concerned with the plight of agricultural workers. Realist artists painted ordinary life and working people, rather than famous people, incidents from history and Classical mythology, or scenes from the Bible. During the 1890s Pellizza was influenced by the Pointillist style of painting. Pointillism was pioneered by the artist Georges Seurat and is a technique in which dots of unmixed color are placed next to each other on a white background so that from a distance they fuse into different colors and tones. Pellizza explored and developed this technique in his paintings in order to soften colors and light to produce an almost shimmering landscape.

Flowers in a Meadow was part of a series called *Idyll*. The theme of the series is love. Besides using Pointillism, Pellizza used symbolic imagery to show the relationship between the cycle of the seasons and the cycle of human existence. The painting is suffused with light that takes on a spiritual dimension. The flowering hedge that the children kneel in front of is symbolic of the blossoming of their young lives, and the light in the sky is the light of hope for tomorrow. The whole composition makes a circle, suggesting the cyclical nature of life.

Flowers in a Meadow

Artist	Giuseppe Pellizza da Volpedo
Nationality	Italian
Painted	*c.*1898–1901

Think about. . .

Pellizza used a technique called Pointillism. What effect does this technique have on the mood of the painting?
The colors and the light appear softened, giving a tranquil mood to the painting.

The figures of the two children seem very blurred. Was there a reason for this?
Pellizza wanted to show the children as part of nature, blending into the landscape.

The painting seems to be made up of lots of circles. Was there a reason for this?
Pellizza wanted to remind us of the cyclical nature of life and the seasons.

Project **Clay candleholder**

One of the most striking aspects of Pellizza's painting is the beautiful flowering hedge behind the children, which has an almost lace-like pattern. In this next project, we will create a clay candleholder with a lace-like pattern pressed through the clay. When a small tealight is placed inside the holder and lit, it will flicker through the wall of the candleholder, highlighting its pattern, and creating a beautiful effect.

1 Find a cup that your tealight fits into. Use this cup as a guide for the size of the candleholder.

4 Turn the cup upside down and cover it with plastic wrap. Drape the clay over the bottom end of the cup and press the clay against the sides of the cup to mold it into shape.

2 Work the clay into a ball.

3 Roll out the ball of clay to a thickness of about ½in (1.25cm).

5 Take your pencil and start to make different-sized holes around the wall of the candleholder. Remove your candleholder from the cup. Put it in the oven to bake for about 30 minutes (check the packet for baking instructions). Allow to cool.

6 Paint inside your candleholder. When the paint is dry, finish with a coat of PVA glue. When the glue is dry, place your tealight candle inside the holder and light.

Top tips

• Make sure you leave enough room at the top of your holder to fit the candle inside—don't forget that clay shrinks when it dries.

• If you don't have a rolling pin, you could use a plastic cup instead.

Project **Nature picture**

In this project we will recreate *Flowers in a Meadow* using a variety of materials. The pastel shades of the background will be strips of tissue paper and the lacy hedge will be made out of doilies. Capture the figures of the children as silhouettes with construction paper.

1 Measure and mark up a border on your construction paper of about 1in (2.5cm) all around. Cut the border out to make a frame, but keep the central rectangle of paper.

2 Cut or tear strips of tissue paper long enough to go horizontally across the frame. Glue the strips in overlapping horizontal bands, gluing the ends onto the edges of the frame.

You will need

A sheet of black construction paper, 8½ x 11in (A4) or bigger

A pencil

A ruler

A pair of scissors

A selection of tissue paper in shades of blue, green, and purple to match Volpedo's painting

A glue stick

Two doilies

3 Cut the lacy bits off the doilies and stick them from the bottom to halfway up the tissue. Tuck the ends under the frame.

4 With the remaining construction paper, draw and cut out the two children in silhouette and stick them down on top of the doily hedge.

Top tip

If you don't want to draw your own figures, photocopy and enlarge the figures in the painting on page 85, and use them as a template.

Artist biographies

Barent Avercamp

1612/13–1679

Dutch

Barent Avercamp was the nephew of Hendrick Avercamp (1585–1634), a famous Dutch artist who specialized in depicting winter landscapes. Barent was probably taught to paint by Hendrick, and for a long time, paintings signed with "Avercamp," or "B. Avercamp," were thought to be by Hendrick, but now, any paintings with either of these signatures, or thought to be painted after 1634 (the year of Hendrick's death), are attributed to Barent. Barent was a merchant, as well as an artist, and, like his uncle, he painted landscapes.

Michelangelo Merisi da Caravaggio

1571–1610

Italian

Caravaggio was an Italian artist. He lived a short and controversial life. But his paintings have influenced generations of artists. His paintings were startlingly realistic to his contemporaries, who were used to the exaggerated forms and compositions of Mannerism, the dominant artistic style of the time. Caravaggio painted characters and scenes from Classical myths and legends, as well as saints and stories from the Bible. He used ordinary people as models for his paintings, so his figures from Christianity look just as ugly, unhealthy, or unattractive as everyone else, not idealized and perfect as they were in most paintings of the day. Caravaggio used dramatic light in his paintings. He shifted from bright, illuminating light to areas of dense shadow and darkness very suddenly, with no transitional areas of diminishing light in between. These lighting effects make his paintings emotional, exciting, and full of action.

Caravaggio was notorious for his drunken brawling and irresponsible lifestyle, and in 1606, he killed a man during a fight and then fled Rome (the scene of his crime). He spent the next four years on the run, in and out of prison, and getting into fights in many places. The exact details of his death are unknown, but it is thought that he died of a fever at a port in Tuscany. He was on his way to seek a pardon for his crimes. He was thirty-eight at the time of his death, and his body has never been found.

Paul Cézanne

1839–1906

French

Paul Cézanne was a Post-Impressionist painter. This means that he was painting after the Impressionists, and he took the Impressionist style a step further in its development. Cézanne is important in the history of Western painting because the style of his art inspired and influenced the next generation of painters, called the Cubists. He is credited with creating a bridge in painting between the nineteenth and twentieth centuries.

Cézanne was interested in painting the truest elements of nature. He tried to break down the forms of mountains, fields, and trees into planes, lines, circles, spheres, and blocks of color that would reflect their essence. By approaching painting in this way, he hoped that he could make art that would have permanent significance and would be hung in art galleries for many years. Cézanne's technique of painting nature was a direct inspiration for Pablo Picasso (1881–1973) and Georges Braque (1882–1963), the founders of Cubism, the first major art movement of the twentieth century.

Flemish school

15th and 16th centuries

Flanders

Artists who were working in the Low Countries or Flanders, from the middle of the fifteenth century onwards. The Low Countries was the name given to the modern-day countries of Belgium, Luxembourg, and the Netherlands. Flanders is an area now within modern-day Belgium. Artists from this part of Europe usually worked in or around the two main cities of Bruges and Ghent.

Art of the Flemish school came to prominence at the same time as the Renaissance in Italy (fifteenth century), and famous artists of this school include Jan van Eyck (c. 1395–1441) and Hugo van der Goes (c. 1440–c. 1483).

Jacob Peter Gowy

c.1632–1661

Flemish

Jacob Peter Gowy was apprenticed to Sir Peter Paul Rubens (1577–1640) and worked for him for a major commission decorating the Torre de la Parada, King Philip IV of Spain's hunting lodge near Madrid. Rubens did the sketches for *The Fall of Icarus,* and Gowy painted it. *The Fall of Icarus* was displayed in the Torre de la Parada.

Edouard Manet

1832–1883

French

Manet was an important artist. He is most closely associated with Impressionism. Manet is thought of as an Impressionist painter because of his loose painting style and everyday subject matter—people sitting, chatting in cafes and parks, people attending the races, or sitting outside railway stations. Manet did not think of himself as an Impressionist because the Impressionists rejected the official institution of art of the day (called the Salon), but he sought its approval, trying throughout his life to win critical recognition.

Important works include *Le Déjèuner sur l'herbe* (*The Luncheon on the Grass*) (1863), *Olympia* (1863), *A Bar at the Folies-Bergère* (1882), and *The Execution of Emperor Maximilian of Mexico* (1868).

Franz Marc

1880–1916

German

Marc was a German Expressionist painter and a founding member of the *Der Blaue Reiter Almanac*, a publication dedicated to expressing new ideas and attitudes towards modern art. Artists contributing to the almanac, such as August Macke (1887–1914) and Wassily Kandinsky (1866–1944), later became known as The Blue Rider group. Marc liked to depict animals, and he made woodcuts and lithographs as well as paintings. His work made use of bright, primary colors, which he believed had emotional properties that communicated through the artwork. Marc was drafted into the German army during World War I and was killed in action in 1916.

Amedeo Clemente Modigliani

1884–1920

Italian

Modigliani was born into a Jewish family in Livorno, Italy, in 1884 and suffered bad health, particularly tuberculosis, as a child. He trained as an artist in Italy and then moved to France, where he spent the

rest of his working life. Modigliani painted and sculpted in a Post-Impressionist style and made a great many portraits. His work was influenced by the art of non-Western cultures, such as Cambodia and Africa. Modigliani died of poverty and tubercular meningitis at the age of thirty-five.

Giuseppe Pellizza da Volpedo
1868–1907

Italian

Giuseppe Pellizza da Volpedo was an Italian painter who used elements of Impressionism and Pointillism in his work. Pointillism was a style of painting developed by the Post-Impressionist painter Georges Seurat (1859–1891). It involved placing tiny dots of color next to each other so that from a distance, the paint takes on the appearance of an entirely different color. Pellizza da Volpedo painted pictures of rural people and their life on the land. His most famous work is *Il Quarto Stato*, which means the Fourth Estate in Italian, and is about farm workers demanding rights.

Paolo Uccello
1397–1475

Italian

Paolo Uccello was a mathematician as well as an artist, and this can be seen in his work, which always grappled with the mathematical problems of perspective related to painting. Uccello was not a very prolific artist, painting only a few large commissions in his lifetime. His most famous works are the three battle scenes he painted depicting the battle of San Romano. In those pictures, soldiers and horses are set out on a strict perspective grid.

James Abbott McNeill Whistler
1834–1903

American

Whistler was born in Lowell, Massachusetts, and attended the West Point Military Academy. Whistler did not enjoy West Point and grew his hair too long, was shabby on parade, and did not excel academically. He did, however, learn drawing and mapmaking from Robert W. Weir, the historical painter and a member of the Hudson River School of American art. After leaving West Point, Whistler worked as a draftsman, drawing the US coastline for the military. He was bored with this work and drew mermaids and sea creatures in the spaces around the maps. In 1855, Whistler decided to become a painter, and he traveled to Paris where he took a studio, studied art, got into debt, and met the painters Edouard Manet (1832–1883), Gustave Courbet (1819–1877), and Theophile Gautier (1811–1872), as well as the writer Charles Baudelaire (1821–1867). In 1859, Whistler moved to London, which was to be his home for the rest of his life. He now perfected his painting style, working on pictures with a limited range of colors, which gave his compositions an overall tonal harmony. He attempted to paint the harmony that is present in music. Whistler was also influenced by the composition of Japanese prints. His most famous picture is *Arrangement in Gray and Black: The Artist's Mother*, also known as *Whistler's Mother*, and it can be seen in the Musée d'Orsay in Paris.

A

Avant-garde: Innovative art at the forefront of the development of modern art is called art of the avant-garde.

B

Baroque: A style of art that depicts scenes from the Bible and Classical mythology in a very bold and heroic way. Baroque paintings can be large in scale and use rich colors, including gold, to communicate the drama and emotion of a scene. The Baroque style of art flourished from the late sixteenth century to the early eighteenth century. Sir Peter Paul Rubens (1577–1640) painted in the baroque style.

Brancusi, Constantin (1876–1957): Brancusi was a Romanian artist who lived and worked in Paris as a sculptor. Brancusi concentrated on paring down his sculptures of objects, people, and animals into simple and elegant shapes that represented the essence of the subject he was tackling. Some of his most famous sculptures are the group known as *Bird in Space*, sculpted throughout his life, and *The Kiss* (1916).

C

Classical mythology: Stories from the cultures of the ancient Greeks and Romans.

Collage: A picture made from bits of paper and other scraps.

Composition: The arrangement of elements in a picture, such as line, color, and form.

Cubism: An art critic, Louis Vauxcelles, named the Cubist movement by noticing that Cubist pictures were "full of little cubes." The first phase of Cubism was called Analytical Cubism (1908–1912). In Analytical Cubism everyday objects were broken down into basic shapes, taken apart, and put back together to represent an object from lots of different angles at the same time. The second phase of Cubism (1912–1919) was Synthetic Cubism. Synthetic Cubism incorporated collage— bits of newspapers, fabric, and music—into pictures. Synthetic Cubism stuck objects together, rather than pulled them apart.

D

da Vinci, Leonardo (1452–1519): An Italian artist, scientist, inventor, writer, poet, sculptor, botanist, engineer, and musician. Many people think that Leonardo da Vinci was the greatest artist of the Renaissance because his interests spanned the arts and sciences and his accomplishments ranged from drawing to plans for weapons of war, such as the helicopter and the tank, to painting masterpieces such as *The Last Supper* (1498) and the *Mona Lisa* (1503–05/07).

E

Etching: A way of making a picture on paper with ink that can be copied many times. The image is cut with acid into a sheet of copper metal, called a plate. The plate is covered in ink, and the ink is then wiped off. The ink stays in the lines that have been cut into the plate. A damp sheet of paper is placed on top of the plate, and the plate and paper are put into a press. The ink in the cuts is transferred to the damp paper while it is pressed, producing a print. This process is then repeated.

F

Futurism: An Italian art movement of the early twentieth century that produced paintings, sculptures, textiles, ceramics, interior design, literature, architecture, music, and industrial design. The Futurists were led by Filippo Tommaso Marinetti (1876–1944), a writer who laid out the principles of the movement in the *Futurist Manifesto*, first published in 1909. The Futurists hated the art of the past and were interested in all of the wonders of the modern industrial age, such as speed, machines, aeroplanes, cars, and motorcycles. The Futurists believed that youth and violence should be praised above all the achievements of the past. Umberto Boccioni (1882–1916), Carlo Carrà (1881–1966), Giacomo Balla (1871–1958), and Gino Severini (1883–1966) were important Futurist artists.

G

Gauguin, Paul (1848–1903): One of the most influential and important Post-Impressionist painters, Paul Gauguin, was a French artist who produced oil paintings, drawings, woodcuts, and engravings. Gauguin was influenced by Impressionism (Gauguin knew Camille Pissarro (1830–1903), Paul Cézanne (1839–1906), and Vincent van Gogh (1853–90)) but felt that it was too superficial a style. Gauguin's work was more symbolic than the Impressionists' work, and he was further influenced by folk art, Japanese art, and African art. In 1891, Gauguin traveled to Tahiti and Polynesia where he painted local people and landscapes until his death there in 1903.

German Expressionism: Several movements in art, architecture, theater, music, and cinema that emanated from Germany in the 1920s and 1930s form the German Expressionist movement. Expressionism tried to communicate the essence of being alive, both emotionally and physically, rather than exactly reproducing what things looked like.

Japanese art: Woodblock prints from Japan were imported into Europe in large numbers during the nineteenth century. These prints influenced European artists who copied their compositions and use of color and line. Other Japanese arts and crafts, such as porcelain, ivory carving, silk, and furniture, also influenced artists, photographers, and designers.

K

Kandinsky, Wassily (1866–1944): Russian artist who is widely acknowledged as the first painter to create completely abstract works of art. An abstract picture doesn't look anything like objects, people, or things. Kandinsky was a co-founder of The Blue Rider group, taught at the Bauhaus, an influential German art school, formulated theories about the emotional and physical significance of colors, and analyzed elements of paintings, such as the point and the line.

M

Macke, August (1887–1914): A German Expressionist painter and a member of The Blue Rider group. Macke was influenced by Impressionism, Cubism, and Futurism. He was killed in World War I, at the age of twenty-seven.

P

Perspective: The skill of being able to draw or paint an object on a two-dimensional surface, such as a piece of paper, so that it looks three-dimensional. During the Renaissance, artists worked out mathematical formulas for perspective.

Pointillism: A style of painting developed by the Post-Impressionist painter Georges Seurat (1859–1891). Pointillism was a painstaking style of painting that involved placing tiny dots of color next to each other so that from a distance the paint takes on the appearance of an entirely different color.

Picasso, Pablo (1881–1973): A Spanish painter and sculptor who is widely accepted as the greatest artist of the twentieth century. Picasso co-founded Cubism with Georges Braque (1882–1963), and pioneered abstract painting.

Pisarro, Camille (1830–1903): A French painter who was an important follower of Impressionism and is significant in his role as a mentor to the important Post-Impressionist artists Paul Cézanne (1839–1906) and Paul Gauguin (1848–1903).

Pop art: A mainly British and American art movement of the 1950s that used mass-produced popular images, such as those commonly found in advertising, and commercial techniques to make high-brow art. Famous Pop artists include Eduardo Paolozzi (1924–2005), Peter Blake (b.1932), Andy Warhol (1928–1987), Jasper Johns (b.1930), Robert Rauschenberg (1925–2008), and Roy Lichtenstein (1923–1997).

R

Realist: A style of painting that originated in France in the nineteenth century and that aimed to depict exactly what the artist had seen. The Realists painted ordinary things, such as rural life and working people, rather than famous people, incidents from history and Classical mythology, or scenes from the Bible. The Realists painted in a rough style, applying the paint in a way that was meant to indicate that they had seen the thing they were depicting.

Rubens, Sir Peter Paul (1577–1640): A Flemish painter who created work in the Baroque style, but was also an academic and a diplomat. Rubens painted religious subjects, portraits of European royalty, self-portraits, scenes from Classical mythology, and stories and incidents from the Bible in a dramatic and energetic style. Rubens ran a large workshop of apprentices who finished works he drew. Rubens also created tapestries and prints.

S

Seurat, Georges (1859–91): French artist Georges Seurat invented a new style of painting called Pointillism, or Divisionism, where tiny dots of color are painted next to each other, which, from a distance, take on the appearance of different colors. Seurat painted *A Sunday Afternoon on the Island of La Grande Jatte*, (1884–1886), in his Pointillist style— it measures 10 feet (3m) across and took him two years to complete—and it has become one of the most famous pictures of the twentieth century. *A Sunday Afternoon on the Island of La Grande Jatte* can be seen at the Art Institute of Chicago. Seurat died at the age of thirty-one.

V

van Gogh, Vincent (1853–90): A troubled Dutch Post-Impressionist painter, famous for his bouts of mental illness, for cutting off a part of his left ear, for having a volatile friendship with Paul Gauguin, and for his lack of success during his lifetime. Van Gogh taught himself to paint and sometimes worked at a furious pace, creating a work a day toward the end of his life. Van Gogh committed suicide at the age of thirty-seven.

Where to see the art in this book

Edouard Manet, *The Balcony* Musée de Louvre, Paris, France

Unknown artist, *The Rainbow Portrait* Hatfield House, England, UK

Amedeo Modigliani, *Portrait of Anna Zborowska* Galleria d'Arte Moderna, Milan, Italy

Barent Avercamp, *Winter Landscape* Hamburger Kunsthalle, Hamburg, Germany

Paul Cézanne, *Mont Sainte-Victoire* The Detroit Institute of Arts, Detroit, USA

James Abbott McNeill Whistler, *Nocturne in Blue and Silver* Museum of Fine Arts, Boston, USA

Paolo Uccello, *St. George and the Dragon* National Gallery, London, UK

Flemish School, *Head of Medusa* Uffizi Gallery, Florence, Italy

Jacob Peter Gowy, *The Fall of Icarus* Museo del Prado, Madrid, Spain

Michelangelo Merisi da Caravaggio, *The Supper at Emmaus* National Gallery, London, UK

Franz Marc, *Im Regen (Under the Rain)* Städtische Galerie im Lenbachhaus, Munich, Germany

Giuseppe Pellizza da Volpedo, *Flowers in a Meadow* Galleria d'Arte Moderna, Rome, Italy

Index

avant-garde 24, 93
Avercamp, Barent 32, 90

The Balcony (Manet) 12–13, 95
baroque 64, 93
box sculpture 40–41
Brancusi, Constantin 24, 93

candleholder, clay 86–87
Caravaggio 72, 90
Cézanne, Paul 38, 90
Classical mythology 58, 64, 84, 93
clay candleholder 86–87
collage 93
collage portrait 26–27
composition 38, 76, 84, 93
Cubism 78, 93

da Vinci, Leonardo 58, 93
Der Blaue Reiter (Blue Rider) 78
drawing, sight 76–77

Elizabeth I, Queen 18–19
etching 44, 93

face shaping 28–29
The Fall of Icarus (Gowy) 64–65, 95
Flemish School 58, 64, 91
flip book 68–69
flowers, giant 80–81
Flowers in a Meadow (Pellizza)
    84–85, 95
frame 22–23
fruit, fabulous 74–75
Futurism 78, 93
Futurist scene 82–83

Gauguin, Paul 78, 93
German Expressionism 78, 93
Gowy, Jacob Peter 64, 91

Head of the Medusa 58–59, 95

Icarus 64–65
Im Regen (Under the Rain) (Marc)
    78–79, 95

Japanese art 12, 44, 94
Japanese painting 48–49

Kandinsky, Wassily 78, 94

landscape 30–49
light and shade 70–89

Macke, August 78, 94
Manet, Edouard 12, 91
Marc, Franz 78, 91
mask, Medusa 60–61
medallion picture 36–37
misty scene 46–47
Modigliani, Amedeo 24, 91–92
monchrome Medusa 62–63
Mont Sainte-Victoire (Cézanne)
    38–39, 95
mosaic dragon 56–57
myths and legends 50–69

nature picture 88–89
Nocturne in Blue and Silver
    (Whistler) 44–45, 95

oil painting 20–21

paint splattering 46–47
painting projects 20–21, 28–29,
    36–37, 42–43, 48–49
papier mâché projects 60–61,
    74–75
Pellizza da Volpedo, Giuseppe 84, 92
perspective 32, 38, 72, 94

Picasso, Pablo 24, 94
picture box 14–15
Pissarro, Camille 38, 94
Pointillism 84, 94
Pop art 94
Pop art project 16–17
Portrait of Anna Zborowska
    (Modigliani) 24–25, 95
portraits 10–29

Rainbow Portrait 18–19, 95
Realist 84, 94
Rubens, Sir Peter Paul 58, 64, 94

sculpture, box 40–41
Seurat, Georges 84, 94
shape a face 28–29
sight drawing 76–77
snow jar 34–35
sponge painting 36–37
St. George and the Dragon (Uccello)
    52–53, 95
stained glass, light and sun 66–67
stencils 46–47
story box, dragon 54–55
string picture 62–63
The Supper at Emmaus (Caravaggio)
    72–73, 95

Uccello, Paolo 52, 92

van Gogh, Vincent 78, 94

watercolor picture 42–43
Whistler, James Abbott 44, 92
Winter Landscape (Avercamp)
    32–33, 95